EXtreme Sports

By Sharon Griggins

Contents

Extreme Sports

Can you imagine rocketing down a city street at sixty miles per hour, the speed of a car on the freeway, lying on an overgrown skateboard just inches away from the concrete? How about climbing straight up a frozen waterfall? Or doing a flip on your bike? Or jumping out of an airplane with a snowboard attached to your feet?

Street luging

extreme: Exceeding the ordinary or expected; radical.

Ice climbing

BMX freestyle
riding

Sky surfing

Street lugers, ice climbers, BMX freestyle riders, and sky surfers are part of the growing world of extreme sports. Just like other athletes, they devote a lot of time to practicing and competing in their sports.

Many of these sports have been created only in the past twenty years. Some sports, like street luging, are all about speed and seeing who can go the fastest. Other sports, like BMX freestyle riding and sky surfing, are about style, or who can do the fanciest stunts. Ice climbing competitors must have both style and speed to win.

Biking to the Max

Racing your BMX bike toward the ten-foot-high half-pipe, you bend over low to gain speed. (A half-pipe is a giant U-shaped structure.) You hit the lip of the pipe and zoom up in the air. You hang there for a moment, and then come down, landing hard on your wheels. This is *nothing* like riding around the block!

half-pipe

This freestyle rider catches some air. BMX bikes are built small and tough to fly high and take a pounding. Freestyle riders must wear helmets when they compete.

BMX freestyle riders perform jumps and stunts in the air. They twist and turn their bikes as they come off a half-pipe. Freestylers also do tricks off a box jump, two ramps connected by a flat board, or a dirt jump, a big mound of earth.

dirt jump

box jump

To win a competition, a freestyle rider must receive high scores from judges in these three areas: height of the jump, style, and degree of difficulty.

The stunts and tricks in freestyle biking have funky names such as "candy bar," "nac nac," and "bus driver." These names describe the ways a freestyle rider moves his body and the bike in the air. To learn these moves, riders watch other freestyle riders and practice a lot.

To do these stunts, a BMX freestyle rider has to practice.

And practice.

And practice, until he or she gets it right.

BMX
Freestyle Moves

bus driver: Spin the handlebars around in the air.

candy bar: Put one foot over the handlebars.

nothings: Take your hands and feet off the bike.

superman: Hold the handlebars and stretch your body out above the bike.

Cool Climbing

Ice climbing is like inching your way up a giant icicle. You hold an ice tool in each hand. On your feet you wear crampons, a set of eight spikes that strap onto your boots. You dangle way above the ground on a big, slippery piece of ice.

Ice climbers use ice tools for handholds.

Ice climbers use crampons for footholds.

An ice climber always works with a partner. They use ropes to secure themselves to the ice in case of a fall.

Ice climbers move slowly and carefully so pieces of ice don't fall and hurt them or their climbing partners.

It takes rhythm to climb a frozen waterfall or ice-covered mountainside. Reaching high, the ice climber hammers the tool into the ice. She pulls herself up and hangs by her arms for a moment.

Next she moves her feet up, kicking the spikes of her crampons into the ice for a hold. Resting on her feet, she continues the motion—hammer, hammer, kick, kick, hammer, hammer, kick, kick—on up the ice to the top.

Full-Body Boarding

You start at the top of a steep city street
and race down the course lying on your
back on an extra large skateboard. Speeding
along, almost touching the pavement, it's
nearly impossible to see where you are
going. Is there a finish line down there
somewhere?

For protection, street luge
racers wear full leather
suits, helmets, and gloves.

In street luge racing, luge sleds can reach speeds of up to sixty miles per hour. A street luge pilot steers by shifting his weight on the sled. Pilots put their feet down on the pavement to brake or slow down.

foot pegs

wheels

handlebars

seat pad

head rest

wheels

Street Luge Lingo

banana: A luge rider who wipes out a lot.

chucking bales: Hitting hay bales that line the luge tracks.

drop a hill: Ride a luge course.

flame: When luge wheels catch fire during a high-speed run.

flowing like water: A smooth, even run down a luge course.

Careful! Don't chuck bales! Tight turns in the course are lined with hay bales in case of a crash.

Street luge races are held on winding, hilly roads. Racers go down the course in pairs or in groups of eight or more. Pilots must watch out for other sleds on the course, especially on the turns, to avoid snags (getting hooked onto other luges).

Surfing the Sky

With a snowboard fastened to your feet, you hop to the open door of the airplane. The wind whips your face and pulls at your body. The ground far below looks like a bright green carpet. You jump and start surfing the air.

After jumping out of the plane, you are in free fall, going through the air without a parachute, for about seventy seconds. Your body moves at 125 miles per hour. It takes your breath away!

Sky surfing is performed by a team of two athletes, a sky surfer and a camera flier. The team dives out of a plane flying thirteen thousand feet above the ground.

The sky surfer rides a specially designed surfboard through the air, doing flips, turns, and other stunts. The camera flier stays right alongside his partner, videotaping the jump with a tiny camera fastened to his helmet.

During the first seventy seconds of a jump, sky surfers and their teammates work together to do their trick routines. After that, they need to concentrate on opening their parachutes and landing safely.

Sky-Surfing Competitions

Judges in sky-surfing competitions score teams by watching the camera flier's video. How do you make a really good video of your partner with a camera on your head? It takes lots of practice to get just the right angle.

You have to be an expert skydiver before you try sky surfing. A sky surfer can practice stunts only in a free fall, or for about seventy seconds of each jump. Sky surfers have to complete a lot of jumps to get the training they need.

Sky surfers have an emergency backup chute inside their parachutes.

Now, maybe you're thinking you'll try an extreme sport soon.

Think again! These sports take a lot of skill and practice. People involved in extreme sports say you should start slow. Get the basics down. Find a good teacher. Be safe. Practice a lot. Practice some more.

And have fun!

Index